The Lewis and Clark Expedition

JOHN PERRITANO

Children's Press®
An Imprint of Scholastic Inc.
New York   Toronto   London   Auckland   Sydney
Mexico City   New Delhi   Hong Kong
Danbury, Connecticut

Content Consultant

David R. Smith, PhD
Adjunct Assistant Professor of History
University of Michigan
Ann Arbor, Michigan

Library of Congress Cataloging-in-Publication Data

Perritano, John.
 The Lewis and Clark Expedition / by John Perritano.
  p. cm.—(A true book)
 Includes bibliographic references and index.
 ISBN-13: 978-0-531-20582-2 (lib. bdg.)   978-0-531-21245-5 (pbk.)
 ISBN-10: 0-531-20582-7 (lib. bdg.)   0-531-21245-9 (pbk.)

 1. Lewis and Clark Expedition (1804–1806)—Juvenile literature. 2. West (U.S.)—Discovery
and exploration—Juvenile literature. 3. West (U.S.)—Description and travel—Juvenile literature.
4. Lewis, Meriwether, 1774–1809—Juvenile literature. 5. Clark, William, 1770–1838—Juvenile
literature. 6. Explorers—West (U.S.)—Biography—Juvenile literature. I. Title. II. Series.

F592.7.P467 2010
917.804'2—dc22   2009014183

All rights reserved. Published in 2010 by Children's Press, an imprint of Scholastic Inc.
Published simultaneously in Canada. Printed in China.
SCHOLASTIC, CHILDREN'S PRESS, A TRUE BOOK, and associated logos are trademarks and/or
registered trademarks of Scholastic Inc.

1 2 3 4 5 6 7 8 9 10 R 19 18 17 16 15 14 13 12 11 10   62

Find the Truth!

Everything you are about to read is true *except* for one of the sentences on this page.

Which one is **TRUE**?

T or F The Louisiana Purchase doubled the size of the United States.

T or F Lewis and Clark did not keep any records of their trip.

Find the answers in this book.

Meriwether Lewis's watch

3

Contents

THE BIG TRUTH!

Animals of the Expedition

Fort Clatsop

4 Across the Rockies to the Ocean

How did the explorers survive the most
dangerous part of their journey?

5 Journey's End

What happened after Lewis and Clark
returned from their trip?

The U.S. Congress gave
Lewis $2,500 for the journey.

Lewis and Clark first met in 1795 when they served together in the army.

CHAPTER 1

Beyond the Mississippi River

In 1801, the United States stretched from the Atlantic Ocean in the East to the Mississippi River in the West. Beyond the Mississippi lay a huge **territory** known as Louisiana. The territory was about 828,800 square miles (2,147,000 square kilometers). The land was unknown to most people living in the eastern part of America. President Thomas Jefferson asked Captains Meriwether Lewis and William Clark to explore the territory.

Lewis and Clark's two-year journey covered 8,000 mi. (12,875 km).

Thomas Jefferson was the third president of the United States. He served from 1801 to 1809.

Thomas Jefferson was also an inventor, writer, and scientist.

Men With a Mission

President Jefferson originally asked Lewis to work in Washington, D.C., as his personal secretary. When Lewis arrived on April 1, 1801, he had no idea that he would become one of the nation's first and greatest explorers. The two men had much in common. Both wanted to solve the mystery of what lay beyond the Mississippi River. When Jefferson asked Lewis to explore the Louisiana Territory, Lewis said yes.

America Grows

At the time, France owned the Louisiana Territory. However, President Jefferson was interested in the region for the United States. The East was getting crowded, and people wanted to move westward. The United States paid the French $15 million for the territory. The sale, known as the Louisiana Purchase, doubled the size of the country overnight. Before the sale was final, Lewis began preparing to lead an **expedition** into this unknown land.

This map of the United States shows the huge area of land west of the Mississippi River that was included in the Louisiana Purchase.

Voyage of Discovery

President Jefferson gave Lewis many instructions. The president told Lewis to keep a journal of the plants and animals that he and his men saw during their journey. Jefferson also told Lewis to draw detailed maps of the areas through which he traveled.

Jefferson asked Lewis to search for a water route called the Northwest Passage. No one knew if such a route really existed. If it did, Jefferson hoped traders and settlers could use the passage to shorten their journey between the Atlantic Ocean and the Pacific Ocean.

Lewis's drafting tools are displayed at the Missouri History Museum.

Meriwether Lewis used these drafting tools to draw maps and sketches of the things he saw along the route.

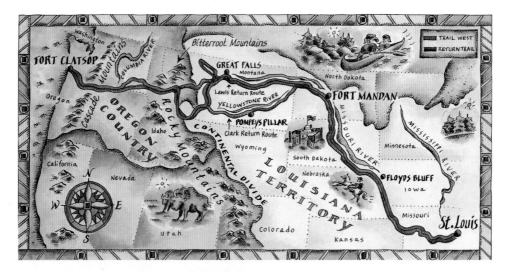

The red line on this map shows the route Lewis and Clark took on their journey west. The blue line shows their return route.

Clark Joins the Team

Lewis asked President Jefferson to appoint William Clark, a soldier, as his second captain. In July 1803, Lewis went to Pittsburgh, Pennsylvania, to prepare for the expedition. He and Clark met on the Ohio River three months later, in October. Their route would take them down the Ohio to the Mississippi River, where their journey would begin.

Lewis, Clark, and the Corps of Discovery left Pittsburgh, Pennsylvania, on August 31, 1803.

CHAPTER 2

Put to the Test

Captains Lewis and Clark headed down the Ohio River to the Mississippi River. Then they turned northwest to the Missouri River. By that time, word had spread that the captains were looking for more men to join their group. Lewis and Clark called the group the Corps (KOR) of Discovery. Together they would face many challenges. They had no accurate maps, and the **terrain** ahead would be rough. They would also be meeting some Native American tribes for the first time.

The Corps of Discovery traveled in three boats.

Into the Unknown

The Corps of Discovery would travel on foot, by boat, and on horseback. On May 14, 1804, the corps set sail up the Missouri River from its camp near St. Louis. The town's residents cheered as the men boarded the boats. The Corps of Discovery included Lewis, Clark, and about 38 other men. They brought along food, **muskets**, knives, a compass, and other supplies. Lewis also brought his dog, named Seaman.

Lewis bought this compass for $5.

Lewis and Clark's compass is on display at the Smithsonian Institution in Washington, D.C.

The men of the corps row their boats to travel up the river.

Mastering the River

The corps' difficult route took them upstream against the Missouri River's **current**. The men had to row the boats or use long poles to push off from the river bottom. Rocks and fallen trees in the river, along with thousands of mosquitoes, made the job harder.

By the spring of 1804, the corps had traveled through what are now the states of Missouri, Kansas, Nebraska, and Iowa. When they weren't rowing, the men hunted and fished for food.

**Peter Gass, a member of the corps, drew this sketch
of Lewis and Clark meeting Native Americans.**

Meeting Native Americans

Lewis and Clark knew they would see Native
Americans on their journey. Yet they had no idea
what these people would be like. The Native people
didn't know if the corps had come to take over their
land and if they would need to fight to protect it.
To make friends with the Native people, Lewis gave
them gifts such as fishhooks, knives, and blankets.

On August 2, 1804, Lewis and Clark met members of the Missouri and Oto (OH-toe) tribes for the first time. However, the Missouri and Oto did not understand English. The tribe members brought along a French trader who spoke English and **translated** their words. As a sign of their friendship, the captains greeted the Native Americans with gifts of tobacco, pork, and flour.

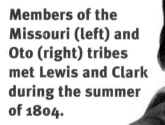

Members of the Missouri (left) and Oto (right) tribes met Lewis and Clark during the summer of 1804.

Fort Mandan

In October 1804, the Corps of Discovery reached present-day North Dakota. There they met the Mandan (MAN-dan) and Hidatsa (hee-DAHT-suh) tribes. Since winter was coming and travel on the frozen Missouri River would be difficult, the captains and their men spent the season with the Mandan.

The corps built Fort Mandan near one of the Mandan villages. It was there that Lewis and Clark met the French-Canadian fur trader Toussaint Charbonneau (too-SAUN shar-bone-OH) and his young wife, Sacagawea (sak-uh-juh-WEE-uh). The captains hired Charbonneau as an **interpreter** (in-TUR-pruh-tur).

The corps stayed at Fort Mandan from November 1804 to April 1805. This reconstruction of the fort is open to visitors.

18

Friend and Helper

After meeting Sacagawea, Lewis and Clark wanted her to accompany them on their journey and talk to Native Americans they might meet. The captains thought Sacagawea could also help the corps trade with Native Americans. Since Sacagawea knew the land well, she helped Lewis and Clark find their way through dangerous territory. She also collected plants and berries for the corps to eat.

During the journey, Sacagawea was reunited with her long-lost brother.

19

After leaving Fort Mandan, the corps continued its travels along the Missouri River.

CHAPTER 3

Deep into the Wilderness

The corps spent five months at Fort Mandan. By April 1805, the Missouri River was no longer frozen. The captains ordered the largest boat, a **keelboat**, and a party of men back to St. Louis to update President Jefferson about their journey so far. The men carried with them examples of animals and plants that most Americans in the East had not seen before.

Lewis and Clark documented 178 kinds of plants and more than 100 types of animals. ➡️

Bobcat

Across the Great Plains

By the summer of 1805, the rest of the corps had struggled up the Missouri River. They reached the Great Plains of what are now North Dakota and Montana. The plains were wide open with miles of grassland. The explorers saw animals they had never seen anywhere else. Clark came face-to-face with a grizzly bear. He had to kill the animal before it harmed him.

Corps member Peter Gass drew this sketch of Lewis, Clark, and other members of the corps shooting bears.

It took the corps one month to build wagons that could carry their supplies around the Great Falls.

A Big Obstacle

On June 13, 1805, Lewis and Clark reached Montana and saw the Great Falls of the Missouri River. Lewis wrote in his journal that the waterfalls were about 600 feet (183 meters) long and 80 ft. (24 m) high. They were beautiful, but a huge obstacle. The explorers had to carry their boats and supplies 18 mi. (29 km) around the falls. Finding the falls proved to Lewis and Clark that the Northwest Passage did not exist.

Animals of the Expedition

President Jefferson had ordered Lewis and Clark to collect information about animals so that people moving west would know what to expect. The captains described more than 100 kinds of animals in their journals.

Prairie Dogs

The French fur trappers who had visited parts of the Louisiana Territory saw an animal they called *petit chien*, or "little dog." Today, it's called the prairie dog.

Bison

Bison were the main food source for the Plains Indians. The corps also hunted bison for food.

Coyotes

Coyotes were unknown in the territory east of the Mississippi River. The men of the corps called them prairie wolves.

In July 1805, nearly one year after the journey began, Meriwether Lewis got his first view of the Rocky Mountains.

CHAPTER 4

Across the Rockies to the Ocean

By July, the Corps of Discovery was about to begin the most dangerous part of the journey—crossing the Rocky Mountains. Sacagawea knew the area well because it was the homeland of her people, the Shoshone (show-SHOW-nee). It was here that Sacagawea helped the corps the most. She convinced the Shoshone to assist the men with finding a route through the mountains.

The Rocky Mountains cover a distance of about 2,000 mi. (3,220 km) from north to south.

The Bitterroot Range is part of the Rocky Mountains.

A flower called the bitterroot grows in the Bitterroot Range.

Crossing the Bitterroot

With help from a Shoshone guide, the Corps of Discovery began making its way through the Rocky Mountains. The corps crossed over the Bitterroot Range, a series of mountains between what are now the states of Montana and Idaho. The 170-mi. (274 km) trek took 12 days to complete.

Meeting the Nez Perce

As they crossed the Bitterroot Range, the corps had difficulty finding food. Since they did not have proper shelter, the days and nights were cold.

When Clark and some men went to look for food, they found a camp of Nez Perce (NEZ PURSE) Indians. The Nez Perce gave them food such as salmon and the root of a plant called camas (KAM-uhs). Clark brought the food back to camp.

The Nez Perce (which means "pierced nose" in French) helped the corps members survive rough conditions in the mountains by giving them food and other supplies.

The Nez Perce offered the men of the corps foods such as dried buffalo, camas, and fish. Since the men of the corps had never eaten these things before, they became sick.

Some of the Nez Perce looked on Lewis and Clark as enemies because they weren't sure what these men wanted. When the members of the corps became ill from eating unfamiliar food, the Nez Perce thought about killing the weakened men. Then they could use the corps' weapons against other tribes. However, a young Native woman named Watkuweis (wah-koo-ICE) convinced the Nez Perce not to harm the men.

To the Columbia

The tribe nursed the men back to health and showed them how to get to the Columbia River. The Columbia would take them to the Pacific Ocean. Some parts of the corps' journey on the upper Columbia were dangerous. They had to steer their boats around sharp rocks and through powerful white-water rapids.

The Columbia River is the largest river in the American Northwest.

The corps reached the Pacific Ocean on November 15, 1805.

The Pacific Ocean in View

When the explorers reached the lower part of the Columbia, their journey got easier. Dry land gave way to green forests. On November 7, 1805, the Corps of Discovery sailed into the **mouth** of the Columbia River.

Eight days later, the tired men arrived at the shore of the Pacific Ocean in what is now Oregon. Everyone rejoiced. Many of the men celebrated by carving their names on trees.

Fort Clatsop

Since their journey west had ended, many members of the corps were eager to return to St. Louis. However, high winds and driving rain would make their return trip difficult. Most of the men chose to stay in Oregon for the winter. They built a square fort called Fort Clatsop.

Fort Clatsop was the first military fort built in what is now Oregon.

Fort Clatsop was named for the local Clatsop tribe who helped the corps survive the winter.

During the corps' stay at Fort Clatsop, they traded with local Indians. Here, Lewis and Clark trade a blue beaded belt worn by Sacagawea for a robe made out of sea otter fur.

CHAPTER 5

Journey's End

The winter of 1805–1806 was long and dreary, cold and wet. There was little to do. Clark spent his time making maps. Both he and Lewis wrote in their journals. By March 1806, it was time to return to St. Louis. Lewis and Clark needed to tell the president— and the nation—about the great things they had seen.

William Clark drew many sketches of animals in his journal.

Homeward Bound

On their way home, Lewis and Clark decided to explore more of the territory. The corps first retraced the route up the Columbia River and into present-day Idaho. In July, the captains split the group. Lewis and his men traveled north of the Missouri River. Clark's group journeyed south of the river. They agreed to meet a month later where the Yellowstone River meets the Missouri River.

Timeline of the Corps of Discovery

1804 ➡

Lewis and Clark begin their journey from a camp near St. Louis on May 14.

November 1804
Lewis and Clark meet Sacagawea.

Welcome Home!

Lewis and Clark returned to St. Louis on September 23, 1806, more than two years after they left. People crowded on the riverbank to welcome them.

Lewis delivered a letter to President Jefferson. It said that the Corps of Discovery had crossed the **continent** and brought back many animals and plants. They had made friends with many different Native Americans. The men also drew maps and pictures of mountains and rivers. Finally, Lewis reported to Jefferson that the Northwest Passage did not exist.

July
1805
The Corps of Discovery begins crossing the Rocky Mountains. The group reaches the Pacific Ocean in the fall.

1806
In March, the corps begins the trip home. They arrive in St. Louis on September 23.

The Journals

During their journey, Lewis and Clark recorded in journals everything they observed. The two men wrote constantly about animals, plants, and the hazards they faced. They made thousands of scientific observations. The journals contained maps as well as drawings of the animals they found. From the journals, Americans got their first look at what lay beyond the Mississippi River. The journals provided valuable information for government officials, settlers, and scientists.

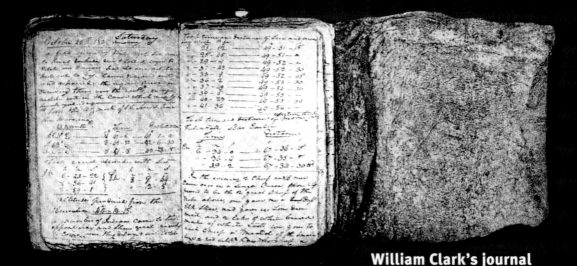

William Clark's journal

Opening the Door to the West

The Corps of Discovery opened the door for others to explore further and settle in the West. John C. Frémont, a soldier, found a route through the Rocky Mountains to Oregon. And former slave James Beckwourth discovered a pass through the Sierra Nevada range that made it easier for people to reach California from the East.

James Beckwourth's pass made travel through the Sierra Nevada range faster and easier.

A New Frontier

Throughout the 1800s, the United States expanded. Now that people knew there were routes they could travel, **pioneers** began moving westward. They believed they would find better lives and more land in the West. Pioneer families loaded their belongings into wagons for a trip that could last as long as two years. Along the way, they built houses and towns. Soon new states and territories were formed and major trade routes, including the Santa Fe Trail, opened.

It took a lot of work to find just a few nuggets of gold.

The discovery of gold in California in 1848 sent thousands of people westward looking for riches.

A wagon train of pioneers heads west.

Leading the Way

The government eventually divided the Louisiana Territory into 15 states, including Wyoming, Montana, Colorado, North Dakota, and South Dakota. Lewis and Clark's expedition made way for the United States to claim even more land in what are today Oregon and Washington. Lewis and Clark are remembered as the greatest explorers in American history. Their brave journey allowed the country to grow from the Atlantic to the Pacific, just as President Jefferson had hoped. ★

This statue of Lewis (right), Clark, and Seaman the dog honors the journey of the Corps of Discovery.

True Statistics

Size of the Louisiana Territory: 828,800 sq. mi. (more than two million sq km)

Price paid for the Louisiana Territory: $15 million

Amount of supplies Lewis and Clark took with them: 44 barrels of pork, 4 barrels of biscuits, and 193 pounds (88 kilograms) of dried soup

Number of gifts for Native Americans: 50 different kinds, including knives, scissors, and fishhooks

Total distance the Corps of Discovery traveled: 8,000 mi. (12,875 km)

Length of time the expedition took: More than two years, from May 14, 1804, to September 23, 1806

Number of states carved out of the Louisiana Purchase: 15

William Clark's journal

Did you find the truth?

T The Louisiana Purchase doubled the size of the United States.

F Lewis and Clark did not keep any records of their trip.

Resources

Books

Fradin, Judith Bloom, and Dennis B. Fradin.
The Lewis and Clark Expedition (Turning Points
of U.S. History). New York: Marshall Cavendish
Benchmark, 2008.

Isserman, Maurice, and John S. Bowman
(editors). *Across America: The Lewis and Clark
Expedition* (Discovery and Exploration).
New York: Facts On File, 2005.

Johmann, Carol A., and Michael P. Kline. *The
Lewis & Clark Expedition: Join the Corps of
Discovery to Explore Uncharted Territory.*
Charlotte, VT: Williamson Publishing, 2003.

Lasky, Kathryn. *The Journal of Augustus Pelletier:
The Lewis and Clark Expedition, 1804* (My
Name Is America). New York: Scholastic, 2000.

Lourie, Peter. *On the Trail of Sacagawea* (Lewis &
Clark Expedition). Honesdale, PA: Boyds Mills
Press, 2001.

Patent, Dorothy Hinshaw. *Animals on the Trail with
Lewis and Clark.* New York: Clarion Books, 2002.

Webster, Christine. *The Lewis and Clark Expedition*
(Cornerstones of Freedom, Second Series). New York:
Children's Press, 2003.

Organizations and Web Sites

Lewis & Clark Fort Mandan Foundation

www.lewis-clark.org/

Read sections of the captains' journals, and trace the route of the Corps of Discovery.

National Geographic Kids: Go West Across America with Lewis & Clark

www.nationalgeographic.com/west/

Play a game as you lead your own expedition across the continent.

PBS: Lewis and Clark

www.pbs.org/lewisandclark/

Take a unique look at the Lewis and Clark expedition.

Places to Visit

Lewis and Clark Boat House and Nature Center

Bishop's Landing
1050 Riverside Drive
St. Charles, MO 63301
(636) 947-3199
www.lewisandclarkcenter.org/

View Native American displays and exhibits about the Corps of Discovery.

Lewis and Clark Interpretive Center

4201 Giant Springs Road
Great Falls, MT 59405-0900
(406) 727-8733
www.fs.fed.us/r1/lewisclark/lcic/

Find out more about Lewis and Clark's long journey.

Important Words

continent – one of the seven large landmasses of the earth. The United States is located on the continent of North America.

current – the flow of water in a river or stream

expedition – a journey taken by a group of people for a reason

interpreter (in-TUR-pruh-tur) – someone who translates one language into another language

keelboat – a bargelike boat with a sail and a rudder that is used for steering

mouth – the place where a river runs into a larger body of water

muskets – heavy guns with long barrels

pioneers – people who are among the first to do something or live in a place

terrain – ground or land

territory – an area or region of land that belongs to and is governed by a country

translated – changed into the words of another language

Index

About the Author

John Perritano is an award-winning journalist and author of many nonfiction titles for children, including books on American history. He holds a master's degree in U.S. history from Western Connecticut State University. He is a former senior editor at Scholastic. He lives in Southbury, Connecticut, with his corps of three dogs, three cats, and three frogs. He has written other True Books, including *The Transcontinental Railroad* and *Spanish Missions*.